IMPRESSIONS FOR EXPRESSIONS

IMPRESSIONS FOR EXPRESSIONS

Poetry that will convey your love

STEVEN GARRETT

attention2detailsmg.com

Contents

1 Significant Other/ Lover   1

2 Family   39

3 Valentines   60

4 Misc./Friend   74

About The Author   86

I

Significant Other/ Lover

" For Eternity "
The image of your beauty
is burnt into my mind
and my heart !
It has been implanted in
My soul from the very
first moment I saw you and
I prayed that one day we
would never want to be apart!
That we would one day be locked
in love blessed by the very soul of God
He would join our souls together
for eternity!
We will be joined in spirit
whenwe leave this earth
to continue on our loving journey!
You are the first thought
in my mind as I awaken each day
as well as the last thought as I fall
asleep every night!
I promise to honor, respect, and to
forever love you with all my might!

" Burning Desire"
You give me a burning
    desire to be the man
    you need me to be!

To give you my heart,
    mind, and soul
        completely!

Your beauty is flawless
    and your loyalty seals
        the deal!

I thank God you are in
    my life for real!

My Queen I truly
    don't think you
        have a clue!

From the depths of My
    soul I will forever
        Love You!

"Flopping Around"
There I was flopping
  around with just
    one wing!

When I flopped into
  you I knew it would
    be more than just
      a fling!

You like me only
  had only one wing
    just like me!

I knew I didn't flop
  into you by chance
    it was destiny!

Our two hearts became
    one and now we
      can fly together!

You are my wing mate
  and I will forever
    Love You!

" Reflection "

As I look at the reflection
   that I now cast over
     the last few years of
        of my life!

I can honestly say I
   am starting to love
   the man in the mirror!

I am going to rededicate
   myself to you my
              wife!

All the changes in my life
   has made the path to
     success so much clearer!

To be the husband, Father,
and Son everyone needs
            me to be!

My Queen thank you
   for sharing your
      life with me!

"Stole My Heart"

Your beauty takes my
 breath away but
Your loyalty stole my
       heart!

My Queen thank you
for not letting anything
      tear us apart!

You are amazing
 absolutely one of
      a kind!

I thank God everyday
 he made you
      mine!

I truly don't think
    you have a
       clue!

From the depths of
   my soul I will
  forever love you!

" Lonely "

Lonely days and
   lonely times!

Not a minute goes
   by that your not
      on my mind!

I thank God I finally
   found my Queen
      at last!

I will never leave
   you like this again
once this time has
      passed!

You are my everything
   a true Queen!

I will forever love
   you with every
   fiber of my being!

" YOU "
You are the light that
   shines upon my path!
      my path!

You are the reason
  My soul can smile
        and laugh!

You are the reason
   that I can trust in love!

You were the one sent to

me from the Lord above!

You are amazing
 You are strong!

You are my rock when
  when things go wrong!

You stood by my side
` through all these
struggles and the strife!

You will forever be loved, honored
   and respected my wife!

" Your Faithfulness "
Your faithfulness is the
beacon that guides
        me home!

The beat of your heart
    is my metronome!

Your loyalty lets me
    know that your
        love is pure!

The peace, love, and
security I have in life is
    because of you for sure!

For this I thank you and know
    in your heart my dedication,
    loyalty, and honor will always hold true!

With every beat of my
        heart I will
    forever love you!

" Make Me Whole "
My soulmate
My confidant
and My bestfriend!

We will be joined in
heaven once our time
on earth ends!

From being kids to
making kids it is
you that has made me
feel whole!

When I am not
with you I am
missing a piece of
my soul!

My Queen yes you
are my everything!

I will forever love
you with every fiber
of my being!

"Keeper of My Heart"

You are the keeper
   of my heart My
      Queen!

You are the mate
   to my soul yes
      My everything!

I thank God every day
   that he brought
   you into my life!

Then I thank him again
 for you saying yes
   to becoming my wife!

I don't think you
even have a clue!

That I can't even begin
   to describe the depth
   of my love for you!

" My Unicorn"
Unicorns are rare and
 mythical creatures of
  legendary tales!

Legend has it that
  if you saw one it's beauty
  would make your heart swell!

They are told to have
magical powers of love
    loyalty and luck!

I was never one to
believe in fairytales
and in life I was surely stuck!

Then something magical
happened the veil covering
   my heart was torn!

When you came into my
life I new the legend was true
I had found my unicorn!

" Complete "
I hope and pray
I complete your
    life!

You complete me
so thank you for saying
yes to becoming my wife!

You never have to
worry about me going
    astray!

Your love fulfills
  me in every way!

Every minute of every
hour of every day
you are on my mind!

I will forever love you
until the end
    of time!

" Missing You"
My Queen I don't
think you have a clue
what you mean to me!

Not being able to hold
and kiss you
is driving me crazy!

Words can't describe how
much I am
missing you!

Yes I am
lonely and blue!

 From the depths
of my soul I
will forever
 Love You!

" The Feeling "
The way your heart
was racing when
you got your first
        kiss!

The thrill of catching
your very first fish!

The excitement of waking
up on Christmas day to see what
Santa left under the tree!

The joy of watching your
favorite team make history!

These were the greatest memories
that ever happened to me
but I really don't think
   you have a clue!

That not one of those memories
 come close to the feeling
I got falling in love with You!

" Motivated and Driven "
Every relationship has
it's up's and downs
   that's a given!

It is my love for You
that keeps me motivated
      and driven!

I don't know what our future
holds but I do know that
it's you I want to forever hold!

I know our love
can be beautiful
   truth be told!

It won't be long
until we can wake
up everyday in each
   others arms!

I will forever love
You and keep your heart, mind,
and body free from harm!

" YOUR "
Your eyes Your lips
    Your face!

These are just a few
of the reasons
no one could ever
  take Your place!

Your loyalty Your love
Your attitude Your heart

These qualities you posses
are why no one could
ever tear us apart!

Your gorgeous Your amazing
Your passionate Your precious
Your honest and true!

These and many other reasons
are why I will forever
    Love You!

" FAITH "
Faith = To have an
allegiance and to have
complete trust in someone!

Yes my Queen Ihave faith
in you forall you have done!

You have given
me faith in love again!

I will faithfully be
your husband and
  bestfriend!

I have faith in us to
love each other through thick and thin!

I have faith in our future
that it will be beautiful
even when our time on
earth comes to an end!

My faith in us is true!
So have faith that
I will forever and ever
Love You and only You!

"Sacred place"

I close my eyes
and drift away and
dream about your face!

Your gorgeous eyes Your
luscious lips these
dreams are like a sacred place!

When I wake up and
realize it was all just
    a dream!

It makes me want my
bestfriend and my confidant
so bad I just want to scream!

My Queen I don't
think you know my heart
        beats true!

And that with every beat
of my heart I miss and
        LOVE YOU!

" Can't Wait "

The days and nights blend
together as one!

Without you to hold
the sleep just doesn't
        come!

I miss your gorgeous
smile and your body
is perfect and pretty!

I can't wait to get to
You to play with your
 HELLO KITTY!

You are the keeper
of my heart, soul,
        and mind!

I will forever love you
until the end of time!

" No Words"

There are no words
that can describe
what You mean to me!

There no words
that can describe
Your beauty!

There are no words
 that can describe
Your loyalty!

There are no words
that can describe
Your sincerity!

There are no words
that can describe how
much I Love You honestly!

There are no words
that can describe how
happy I will be to Love You
     for eternity!

"Then You Came into My Life"

Just like Eeyore My life
has always been covered
by clouds of hopelessness
    and despair!

Like I am always about
to fall off of life's
edge and happy days
    were rare!

Then You came into
My life and the clouds
have begun to part and
the sun has started to
shine in my life!

The day I realized I was
not falling off of life's edge
but merely standing on a rock
was the day you said yes
to becoming my wife!

"Eternal"

To know you is like
knowing an Angel in
    the flesh!

You will be my
soulmate even after
    death!

Unlike this life
on earth which
   is passing!

Our love is eternal
  yes everlasting!

Our spirits will soar
together through the clouds
and up into heaven so
that we can thank God
for making us for
    each other!

Then we will rest
in eternal bliss with
  one another!

" More Than Words "

I miss you more
than words can describe!

I know it has been
tough but true love and
friendship always
  survives!

I miss you touch
I miss your smile!

I love that even
now you still always go
that extra mile!

I miss everything
about you my
  Queen!

I will forever
love you with every
fiber of my being!

"Missing Piece"

You make my spirit shout
with joy and my
heart smile with glee!

You are the missing
piece to my puzzle that
    completes me!

You make my world
brighter and took away
      the rain!

You showed me how
it felt to be loved
and took away the pain!

You made me feel
wanted and the
opposite of lonely!

You my Queen are
My one and only!

" More Precious"

You are more precious
than diamonds and
more gorgeous than gold!

You are my eternal soulmate
and I wouldn't change one
thing about you truth
    be told!

You are amazing
You are strong
You are my life!

Words can't truly explain
what you mean
to me my wife!

Thank You for loving
  Me My Queen!

I will forever respect,
honor, and love You
with every fiber of My being!

"Eternal Flame "

My eternal flame
burns for you
My Queen!

Yes You are My
forever yes My
   everything!

Love has always hurt
and I really thought
I would die lonely
     and old!

Then I met you and
Your love brought My
heart out of the cold!

Thank You for showing
me how it feels to be
wanted and cared for too!

My Queen from the
depths of my soul
I will forever Love You!

"Everyday"

Everyday we have together
is a day I can
express my love for you!

My bestfriend My
confidant it is for
you my heart beats true!

Everything in my life
has gotten better since
you came along!

The happiness I feel
the joy you bring
is deeper than every love song!

You are the shining
star that lights my path!

Our love is real and
will forever last!

"One of a Kind"

I want to say
thank you for staying
on this journey with me

You will always hold
a special place in my
heart for all eternity!

So many people have
come and gone I
don't think you
    have a clue!

You though have
stayed loyal and
    true!

You are truly one
    of a kind!

Thanks again for not
forgetting about me
nor leaving me behind!

" Who-Who"

Who! Who!
You!   You!

I've stayed up night
after night searching
  every tree!

Let me check the
lock to your heart
I think I have the key!

Who! Who!
You!   You!

Finally I found the lock
my key would open up so
my search has come
   to an end!

I have found my soulmate,
my confidant, and
   my bestfriend!

Who! Who!
You! You!

" Perfect for ME "

You made me
believe in love when
I thought love was only
        in fairytales!

You make me understand
the verse in the Bible
love never fails!

You complete me and
make me whole!

You breath life back
   into my soul!

You are perfect for
me in every way!

You have my mind,
heart, and soul
   day after day!

" A Puzzle "

 Life has been a
puzzle without the pieces
    to complete it!

I always had a hole
in my heart not finding
the piece that fit!

Not knowing what to do
or where to search!

Tired of forcing pieces
into the puzzle that didn't fit
        always hurt!

Then I found the
piece that fit
   for real!

You are the the piece
that fit and completed my heart
        and let it heal!

" LOVE IS "

Love is more
than just a word!

Love is an action
and a feeling
that means a lot!

Love is everlasting forgiving
and nurturing as
        well!

Love is willing to
compromise and willing
to listen when you
    have something to tell!

Love is selflessness and
    sacrificing too!

This is what love
means to me so
know that I Love You!

" Falling Star "

A falling star that
took my breath away!

I caught that star
with my heart and I
will never let you get away!

Now your star
lights up my
    soul!

It is your star that
makes me whole!
Thank You for
Your shining light!

I love you for making
My life so bright!

" Full Bloom"

Like a rose in full
bloom you have opened
up my heart!

You are my forever and
nothing will ever
  tear us apart!

Thank You for showing
me that love is real and
not just in fairytales!

Compromise, communication, loyalty,
respect, and honor are just a few of
the reasons why love never fails!

You truly are a
    Queen!

I will forever love you
with every fiber of my being!

"I Know"

I just thought you
should know that
    I know!

That I will reap
what I sew!

What I sew is coming
straight from my
        heart!

Just the thought of
not having your lips
to kiss tears me apart!

So I promise to sew love
into that will always
make you feel like a Queen!

I love You and you will
always and forever
be the Lady of my dreams!

"Chapters"

Most chapters in life
have been tales of
  deceit and lies!

Leaving me broken
hearted with tear
  filled eyes!

Tales filled with
loneliness and
   despair!

Chapters filled with
villains and snakes where
I fell deep into a pit and
   didn't even care!

Then I realized I was not
alone in my pit and hope
made my heart start to swell!

You are the newest chapter in
my life and what I thought
was a horror story was
   really a fairytale!

" Loved by You "

There isn't a feeling
I have ever felt that
feels the way I feel
being loved by you!

I have never experienced
a love that was loyal
    and true!

I have never had anyone
make sacrifices for me
like you have made for me!

Thank You for loving
me the way you love
    me!

I promise to always and
always reciprocate your
    love for eternity!

2

Family

"Strive To Be"
Grandmother I want you
  to know that you have
    always inspired me!

You are truly who
  every person should
    strive to be!

You have always put others
    before yourself you have
      always given me hope!

You have always put
others before yourself
You have always given me hope!

I have never heard you
cuss nor have I ever seen
  You drink or smoke!

You are loving, nurturing,
  caring, and you are
You are always positive too!

Grandmother thank you for
  being you and I
    will forever love you!

" Beacon "

You have always been
 a beacon in my life
  guiding me home!

You have always kept me
 on track like the beat
  of a metronome!

You have always been
 the voice of reason
  when I am mad!

You have always been
there to give
 me a hug when I am sad!

You have always loved
 me like no other!

You have always
 been the greatest
  Mother!

" I Am Now Maturing"

Mother I can't put into words
        what you truly mean
                to me!

Thank You for always being
there even when I caused
        You so much misery!

Mother thank you for carrying
    me in your belly and giving
        me a breath of life!

I know it is time to grow
    up and quit living
        in strife!

I am now maturing into
    the man you always wanted
                me to be!

From the bottom of my
    heart I will love you
        for all eternity!

" You Are "

You are amazing
 You are strong!

You are my rock
 when things go
  wrong!

You you gentle
 You are kind!

You have always been
 there and stood the
  test of time!

You are nurturing and
 forgiving you have
loved me like no other!

You are a giver of life
for this I love and
 thank you Mother!

I hope and pray
 You have the happiest
 Mothers Day!

" No Words "

There are no words that
  can describe what you mean
                to me!

There is nothing like a
mothers love for this
statement you are the epitome!

I have lied I have stolen
I have disrespected and
 said hurtful things!

I am sorry Mother
and thank you for the
  hope your love brings!

I am truly trying to mature
into a man and have set
goals to obtain my dreams!

One of my dreams is
to show you I Love You
with every fiber of my being!

" An Angel "

I thank God he gave
  me an angel for
   a mother!

You have always loved
   like no other!

Momma thank you for
  all the sacrifices you
  make for me!

I will forever love
you for all eternity!

Your are the greatest
Mother anyone could
ask for I must say!

Mother I wish you
the happiest of all
  Mothers Day!

" This Special Day "

This special day
 comes only once
    a year!

Truth be told I
 wish I was there!

On this day the Lady
who gave me life was
   given life on this day!

Your strength, faith, love,
compassion, and integrity
are profound in every way!

Mother I love you from
the depths of my soul
and I want to wish you
the happiest birthday!

" I Am Sorry "

I thank God he
gave you me as a
    Mother!

You have always been
there and supported me
when there was no other!

Thank you for sticking
by my side through all
the struggles and strife!

I am sorry for all
the bad decisions I
have made in life!

I am sorry for every tear
I have made you cry from
giving you the blues!

From the depths of my
soul I will forever
    love you!

" Thank You "

Thank You for giving
     me life!

Thank You for supporting
    me through all the struggles
            and strife!

Thank You for loving
me like no other!

Thank You for being
     My Mother!

Thank You for always
 believing in me
and never giving up!

Thank You for everything
      and loving me
     no matter what!

" My Present To You "

This special day
comes only once
       a year!

On this day we celebrate
your life and my
heart draws near!

I want to bring a smile
to your face and joy
   to your heart!

I know my bad decisions
in life have been tearing
          you apart!

My present to you is
maturing into the man
 you have always wanted me to be!

Mother I wish you a
happy birthday and will
love you for all eternity!

" Qualities "

Grandmother love, dedication,
loyalty, patience, forgiveness,
nurturing, and honesty hold true!

All of these words remind
    me of you!

Thank You for always
being thoughtful and
        kind!

Even when I didn't
deserve it most of
        the time!

Thank You for raising
  my mother with
these same qualities to!

From the depths of
  my soul I will
forever Love You!

" Not A Day Goes By "

Mother not a day goes
by that you don't cross
     my mind!

Thank You for all the
sacrifices you make
time after time!

When ever I feel
that life has me
on the ropes!

I think of you because
it is your love that
brings me hope!

Mother I don't think you
       have a clue!

What you mean to me
and how much
 I Love You!

" You Did Your Best "

From the days when
it was rock a bye baby
to put me to sleep!

Until I was a teenager
making choices that made
        You weep!

Mother I am sorry I
didn't mind and and gave
you so much grief and heartache!

Mother just know you did
your best it was my way of
thinking that was the mistake!

I honestly believe you are
perfect mother in
  every way!

From the bottom of my heart
and the depths pf my soul
I Love You and want to
wish you a Happy Mothers Day!

" Sacrifices "

It takes a special kind of
  lady to become a
      mother!

The sacrifices you have
      to make are
      like no other!

So on this day I want
to give you the honor and respect
You deserve as a giver of life!

You are a true Queen
my wife I love you
and hope and hope and pray!

That you have the
Happiest Mothers Day!

" Golden Years "

Mom and Dad
this special day
comes only once a year!

Truth be told
I wish I could
be their!

To see you all
in the glory of
your Golden Years!

Mom and Dad I
want to than you
for always being their!

You both are what
true love is
all about I must say!

I Love y'all and
  wish you a
Happy Anniversary!

" My Little Superman "

I want you to
know you are my
little superman!

I need you to mind
your mother and help
her as much as you can!

I want you to know
   you are in all
    my prayers!

Just because I am not
at home doesn't mean
    that I don't care!

" My Son "

My son my only
one you are growing
into a young man!

I want to give you
a little advice set
goals and make plans!

That way you know
which direction you
want to go in life!

It will save you
a lot of heartache
    and strife!

My son you can always
come to me to get
something off your chest!

Just know I love you and
you are truly blessed!

" I Want You To Know "

My Baby Girl has
grown into a
 young lady!

I missed so much
and for this I
   am so sorry!

I want you to know I
am proud to be
your father baby girl!

You are smart and pretty
and will always be
the Princess of my world!

You truly are
   a star!

Baby Girl you
truly are perfect and
I adore who you are!

" Baby Girl "

It won't be long
until daddy can hold
   you in his arms!

Or tuck you into
bed and keep you
free from harm!

I need you to
be a big girl and
listen to your mother!

You will always be
our Baby Girl there
  will never be another!

I Love You
  Baby Girl!

And know in your
heart you will always
  be Daddies whole world!

" My Whole Life Changed "

The day we met
my whole life changed
for the better!

I thank God every day
that he put
you in my life forever!

You have been a true Queen
to me in my life!

You are truly the
epitome of what it means
to be a wife!

My soulmate, my confidant,
My bestfriend whom means
everything to me!

I love you and
want to wish you
a happy anniversary!

3

Valentines

" Celebrate Love "

This is the day we
celebrate love with
those we love!

Mother you are truly
an angel sent
from the Lord above!

I am sorry I have
caused so much
heartache and pain!

Yet you have never
left my side nor have
you ever changed!

For this I am forever
grateful and am seeking to
mature into a grown up
I know it is past time!

Mother I will forever love
you and want to wish
you a happy valentines!

" My Current State "

When you are down
and out you will
find your true friend!

The one that will
be there through
tick and thin!

In my current state
you don't understand
what that means to me!

In my heart you are
more than just a friend
   you are family!

Just know you are
in my thoughts and
prayers all of the time!

I hope you are having
a great day and I want to
wish you a happy valentines!

" Be Mine "

Be mine not for today not for
tomorrow and not
  just for tonight!

Be mine for all
eternity not just
for this life!

Be mine and I will provide
and protect you with
  all my might!

Be mine, Be mine
  Be mine, Be mine

Be mine not just today
but with you every day
  is valentines!

" Rewind "

Princess I truly Don't
know what all I missed
in this time apart!

But know not a minute
goes by that you
are not in my heart!

Just know if I could
hit a rewind button
I would change a lot of things!

I miss you with
every fiber of my
    being!

Princess I am truly
sorry that I have missed
        all this time!

I love you Baby Girl
 and want to wish You
a happy valentines!

" Mistakes "

My princess I know
I haven't been their like
 a father should be!

I am sorry I made
mistakes and I have
been gone for an eternity!

But don't think I
don't love you or
or that I don't care!

You are forever in my
heart and in
everyone of my prayers!

My Princess you are
all grown up and
one of a kind!

Your father loves you
with all his soul and I
wish you a Happy Valentines!

" Cupid's Arrow "

The minute I saw you
cupid's arrow struck
     my heart!

From that second
I knew nothing would
ever tear us apart!

You are my Queen
yes the lady of my
        dreams!

It is for you and
only you that my
    heart fiends!

Every second of
every minute of every
hour you are on my mind!

My Queen I will
forever love you and
wish you a Happy Valentines!

" Searching "

We spend our lives searching
for the one we can trust
    with our hearts!

Now that I finally
found you i won't let
any thing tear us apart!

You are my soulmate
    My confidant and
      My bestfriend!

You are the keeper
of my soul even
when my time on earth ends!

Your lips taste better
      than fine wine!

From the depths of
my soul I love you and
wish you a Happy Valentines!

" My Little Princess "

My little Princess
I wish I could
tuck you in at night!

My little princess
I wish I could hug
and hold you tight!

My little princess
I love you
with all my heart!

My little princess
I am so proud of how
you are getting so smart!

My little princess
you are always in my
prayers and on my mind!

My little princess
I love you and wish
you a happy valentines!

" Refined "

I prayed for years for God
to put the lady he had
        for me in my life!

I didn't think he heard
but I guess he knew I
wasn't ready for a wife!

I thought I was ready but
had a lot to learn and he put me
through the fire so my love could
                be refined!

Then you came into my
life and I was scared but God
had sent me my Queen and soulmate
I love you and wish you a happy valentines!

" Tilt a Whirl "

You are my girl
the Queen of my
    world!

You got my heart
my head and my soul
in a tilt a whirl!

Your beauty is flawless
and your loyalty seals the deal!

My Queen these
feelings I have for
you are deep for real!

I wish I was their
to look you in the
eyes when I say

I love You and
wish you the
happiest valentines day!

"Anchored"

I was being tossed
around on waves of the
      sea of life!

When I found you
 your love anchored
me down my wife!

Now I have joy,
love, peace, and you
make me smile and laugh!

You my Queen
are my better half!

I want you to know
you are one of a
      kind!

I love you and
want to wish you
a happy valentines!

" Lucky Star "

I want to say
thankyou for staying
loyal and true!

I thank my lucky stars
for a friend
    like you!

When I get stressed
out and the going
      gets rough!

I can count on you
and that is usually
      enough!

Last but not
least I want to say!

Thank you for just
being you and I hope
and pray you have
the happiest valentines day!

" Lady of My Dreams "

To my Queen
the lady of my
  dreams!

It is for you and
only you that my heart
        fiends!

You are my soulmate
my confidant and
my bestfriend!

We will be joined in
heaven when our
time on earth ends!

My Queen know you are
always in my heart
and on my mind!

I love you and wish you
a happy valentines!

4

Misc./Friend

" Freedom To Ride "

Burning up the
highway to the thunder
    of your bike!

The smoky bar rooms
in different cities meeting
new brothers every night!

This is the way we
choose to live
    our lives!

Freedom to ride
where only the
strong survive!

Brother I wouldn't
change a thing
    I must say!

You survived another
year and I wish
you a happy birthday!

" The Fishermen "

Is it just the sense
of peace just being
out in nature?

Is it the thrill of the
adrenaline coursing through
you from the time you set the hook
until you have landed your trophy?

Is it the camaraderie
and the bonds you form
with friends and family?

Is it the stories and
memories to be told
and past down from
generation to generation?

Is it simply the deliciousness
of the catch that brings you
back to the water time and time again?

It is all of
these that make me love
being a fisherman!

" Always Been "

I want you to know
 you are in my thoughts
      and in my prayers!

I truly do miss you
and I truly do care!

You have always been
their through thick
      and thin!

You have always
been a true friend!

Thankyou for being
the person you are!

I miss you with every
bit of my heart my
shooting star!

"What Came First "

Sometime life leaves you
feeling like what came first
the chicken or the egg!

Sometimes you want to
drown away your sorrows
and a six pack won't cut it it
feels like you need the whole keg!

Well my friend in those
times just know you always have
        me to talk too!

I know you are going
through things and I
just want you to
know I was thinking about you!

" Thank You "

Thank you for showing
me I truly have
    a friend!

You have always been
loyal and caring as
friend ever could have
          been!

I don't have many
people I could count
on but you have never
      let me down!

It is you that lifts
my spirits when my
face is wearing a frown!

Thankyou for just
      being you!

What you mean to me
I don't think you
really have a clue!

" Everything is Better "

Everything is better with
    the right friend!

Like walking down the
beach feeling the warmth
of the sun and the coolness
    of the wind!

Laying in the sand
dunes enjoying conversation
    underneath the stars!

Learning to compromise
understanding women are from
Venus and men are from Mars!

Or searching for seashells
until the day light
        ends!

I am so grateful to have
you as such a close
        friend!

" Priceless "

I am sending you
this card to let you know
that you are on my mind!

Thank you for remaining
my friend after all
        this time!

Almost everybody
has wilted away but
you have stayed loyal
        and true!

Your friendship is
priceless and my life
is better just from
 knowing a person like
        YOU!

" A New Family "
We have lived most of our lives in
            turmoil and despair!
Serving the father of lies believing no one really
loved us or for that matter even cared!
Believing the lies that we would never amount
to anything or that our lives had no worth!
Most of these lies and self depreciating abuse
have been preached to us since birth!
So we have become victims of Satan and the world
driven into helplessness, depression, and
                low self esteem!
I am here to tell you that truly you have worth
and are highly regarded, you are loved, and given
new life through The Price of Prince's
            and King of King's!
So I encourage you to serve this new King!
He is the father of hope the giver of love and
through him we can do anything!
So be thankful for the breath of life
you have been given!
You will be a welcome part of this new family
in this new life that you can believe in!
It is a life of faith, hope, and love never
hatred or shame!
So give thanks you have been bought by the
blood and call upon his holy name!
   In Jesus Name Amen and Amen!

" A Convicted Heart "

As I sit back and reflect on my life there is a lot
of hate, shame, turmoil, and despair!
Most of it self inflicted but blaming others out
of embarrassment and fear!
For years I believed I was just not meant to
succeed and content to live a drug addicts life!
The scheming, the stealing, the robbing, and pillaging
until I ended up in prison time and time again!
Until I finally looked in the mirror with eye's full
of tears what looked back at me was my worst friend!
The image looking back at me was truly begging for
a change and that had to start from within!
I had to write everyone I loved that I stole from
and lied to and admit to everyone of those sins!
It was the hardest thing I ever did being honest to the
ones I love telling them how I stole lied and denied
          but this is where I had to start!
Now I am maturing into a man that has integrity
and accountability and I am telling you
       the story of a convicted heart!

" The One Thing "

In life there is one thing you
can never get back!

Most of us have squandered more than
we even realize just not having a
   plan of attack!

Just sitting there without purpose or drive!

Some lost in depression or discontent not even
caring if they were dead or alive!

Others wasting away wandering going
through life doing everything half assed!

If you are going to waste this one resource
in life you can never get back use it wisely
      on something that will last!

You are only given an allotted amount you
never know how much you have so always
tell your loved ones how much you love them
         and what's on your mind!

So make every second count well I got
   to go before I run out of time!

" Time To Fight "

I was discontent like an instrument that
had no one to play it know what I am saying!
In other words useless, clueless, and worthless
        my own self I was betraying!
By believing I was not to blame for my short
comings always having someone else to blame!
The reality is I was the one causing all my
                own shame!
This realization caused a new thought to click
in my brain and it was a true desire to change!
I was a drug addicted liar who stole and lied
and burnt every bridge in my life!
This new desire of change wouldn't let
me throw in the towel no it was time to fight!
It has been the hardest fight I ever fought in
my life learning to love the man in the mirror!
Now after fighting my demons for years the path
to authentic manhood is getting clearer!
It is a path of integrity and accountability as well
as sobriety that created the perfect storm that cleared
all the ashes from the foundation of the bridges that
I burnt in life creating me a new opportunity!
To rebuild bridges with my Mother, Father, Brothers,
and my Son while learning to be a servant leader
                in my community!

Steven Garrett has spent close to 25 years incarcerated. He was addicted to drugs and maintained his addiction by wreaking havoc on his community and those who loved him most in this world. Steven has had many stints in and out of prison and now he dedicates his sobriety and change in his life to Jesus Christ. He is now a published author and entrepreneur giving back to the communities he once was so harmful to. visit attention2detailsmg.com to see Steven's powerful artwork.